Laura Ingalls Wilder

Christi E. Parker, M.A. Ed.

Table of Contents

The Life of a Pioneer Woman 3

A Pioneer Girl Is Born 4–5

Moving West 6–7

Hard Times 8–9

Laura Begins a New Life .10–11

Troubles on the Frontier .12–13

Becoming a Writer 14–15

Pioneer Women
    The First Pioneer Woman 16–17
    A Woman's Life on the Trail 18–19
    Women Living in the West 20–21
    Freedoms for Western Women 22–23

Glossary 24

Index 25

The Life of a Pioneer Woman

Laura Ingalls Wilder grew up in many **prairie** (PRAIR-ee) towns. Her family moved often because life was so difficult. Laura knew **frontier** (fruhn-TEAR) life was hard. But, she loved the prairie. Laura was a farmer, teacher, and writer. She and other pioneer women helped the United States become what it is today.

Laura Ingalls Wilder

▼ Pioneer families resting by their covered wagons

A Pioneer Girl Is Born

Laura Ingalls was born in the "Big Woods" of Wisconsin in 1867. Laura's parents were Charles and Caroline Ingalls. She called them Pa and Ma. She had an older sister named Mary. Charles Ingalls thought the West would offer his family more opportunities. So, the Ingalls family moved to Missouri when Laura was just a baby.

Then, Pa heard about the Homestead Act. This law gave free land to people. This was a great opportunity for farmers who never thought they would own land. The

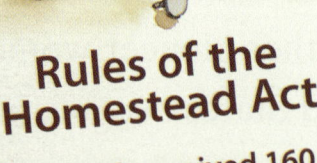

Rules of the Homestead Act

Farmers each received 160 acres of free land. After a farmer lived on a homestead for five years, he had to write a "final proof" in the newspaper. This said that the farmer had lived on the land and farmed it. After this, he got to keep the land.

▼ This is Charles Ingalls' homestead application from 1880.

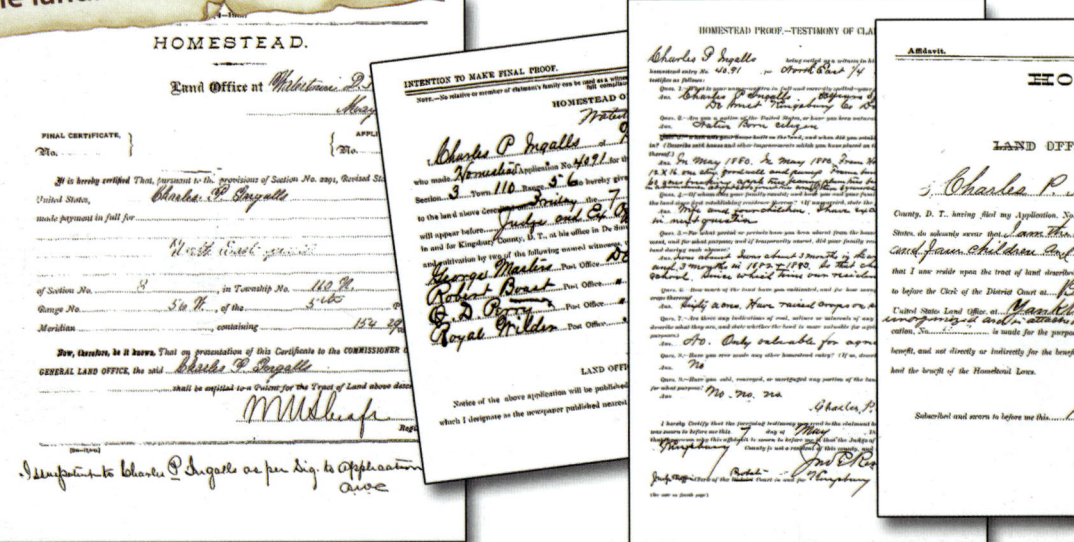

settlers had to farm the land for five years in order to keep it. The Ingalls family moved to Kansas to set up their **homestead**.

Sadly, the family got **malaria** (muh-LAIR-ee-uh). They also started to fear the American Indians in the area. A third Ingalls girl, Carrie, was born. But, life in Kansas was too hard. Pa decided to move back to the East.

Carrie, Mary, and Laura Ingalls ▲

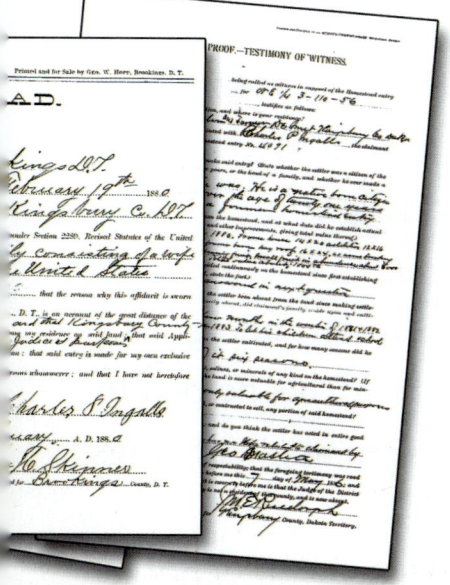

▲ This 1869 picture makes life on the homestead seem perfect. It was rarely this easy.

Meeting Nellie Owens

Laura met Nellie Owens at school in Walnut Grove, Minnesota. She was the daughter of a shop owner. Nellie and Laura were **rivals**. They competed with each other. Nellie became a character in Laura's books about her life. But, her name in the books was Nellie Oleson.

▲ The Ingalls family built their dugout in the side of a creek bank.

Moving West

Charles Ingalls was still not happy in the East. He wanted to move west again. So, the Ingalls family moved to Minnesota. At first, they could not afford a real house. They lived in a **dugout** on the banks of Plum Creek.

Dugouts were made of **sod**, which is mixed dirt and grass. The inside walls were covered with newspaper. This helped to keep rain water out. Roofs of the dugouts were made of twigs, sod, and straw.

Later, Pa bought enough wood to build a cabin. On their farm, the family grew wheat. Then, disaster struck. Swarms of grasshoppers ate their entire crop two years in a row. The family was left in **debt** and had little to eat.

▲ This cabin room is very fancy. The Ingalls' cabin would have had more simple furnishings.

Log cabins on the prairie were nicer and more permanent than dugouts. ▶

Hard Times

In 1875, a baby boy was born into the Ingalls family. Sadly, he lived less than a year. Since living in the West was so hard, it was not uncommon for babies to die.

Once again, it was difficult for Pa to find a job. The family moved to Iowa. Ma and Pa worked in a hotel there. They were not happy living in a city.

They decided to move back to Minnesota. There, Laura's baby sister, Grace, was born. Two years later, Mary became very ill and went blind.

Pa found a job with a railroad company. So, the family moved to the Dakota **Territory** (TAIR-uh-tor-ee). There, Pa filed for a new homestead site near the town of De Smet.

▲ Laura wrote about many of the songs that she remembered from her childhood.

Entertainment During the Rough Winter

Laura enjoyed listening to Pa tell stories at night. He also played music on his fiddle. When Pa died, Laura kept his fiddle.

▲ These cattle are caught in a blizzard on the plains.

The people on the plains called the winter of 1880–1881 "The Hard Winter." It was one of the worst winters in history. **Blizzards** came one after another. The railroads could not get through the large amounts of snow. The pioneers did not get many supplies, including food. The walls of some homes were so thin that people died from the cold. The **livestock** died, too. The Ingalls family was lucky to survive this long winter.

▼ The Ingalls family is listed on this 1880 census from the Dakota Territory.

Laura Begins a New Life

Laura became a teacher when she was 15. The money she earned helped send Mary to a school for the blind in Iowa. Mary was lucky that her family could afford to send her to the school. At that time, most blind people did not have special training to help them succeed.

The school where Laura worked was 12 miles away from De Smet. She had to live near the school during the week. She did not like being away from home.

Laura Ingalls and Almanzo Wilder were married when Laura was 18.

Young Teachers

During the time that Laura was growing up, most married women did not work. Once young women were married, they stayed at home to raise their children and do household chores. This is one reason that girls left school at a young age to become teachers.

A young man named Almanzo Wilder lived near Laura's parents. Every weekend, he traveled to Laura's school and brought her home to her parents. Over the next three years, Laura and Almanzo fell in love.

Laura married Almanzo in 1885. Their daughter Rose was born in 1886. Laura also had a son, but he died as a baby.

▼ Rose Wilder

Why Didn't They Smile?

Times were hard for pioneers. But, that is not why they look so serious in pictures. Cameras were new, and they took a long time to capture an image. Try holding a smile on your face for two minutes. Isn't it easier to look serious?

▼ Wild prairie roses

Troubles on the Frontier

The first few years of Laura and Almanzo's marriage were very difficult. Hail and **droughts** destroyed their crops. Then, a fire burned down their home. Almanzo became ill with **polio** (PO-lee-o). This disease makes people weak and sore. So, working on a farm became even more difficult.

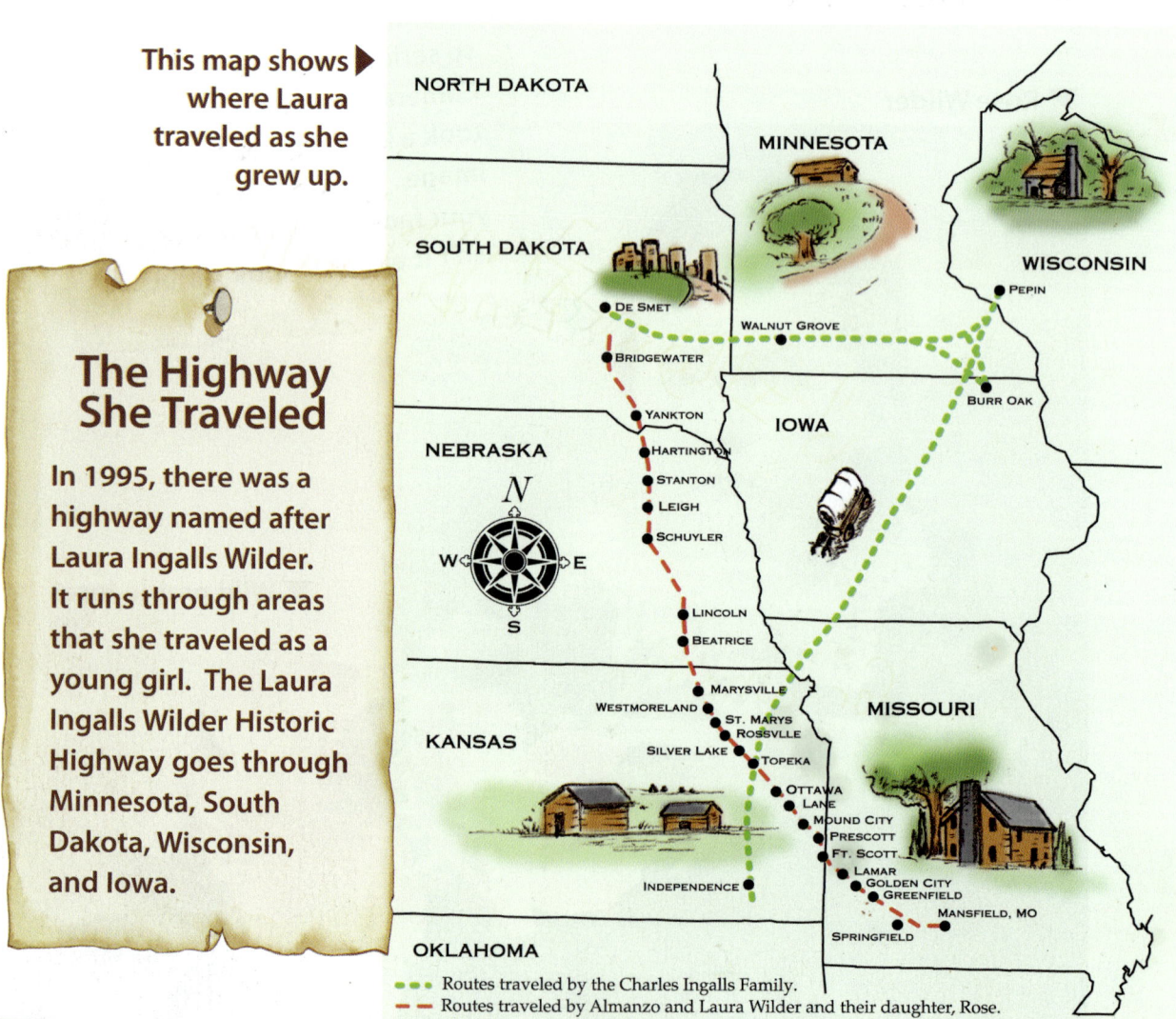

This map shows where Laura traveled as she grew up.

The Highway She Traveled

In 1995, there was a highway named after Laura Ingalls Wilder. It runs through areas that she traveled as a young girl. The Laura Ingalls Wilder Historic Highway goes through Minnesota, South Dakota, Wisconsin, and Iowa.

Laura and Almanzo decided to move and try to find a new way of life. Nothing seemed right for the young family. Finally, they saw the beautiful land of the Ozarks in Missouri. They bought Rocky Ridge Farm. Over the years, they added on to the original farmhouse to build a comfortable home.

To earn money, Laura cooked for railroad men. She also wrote about farm life for the local newspaper. For fun, Laura and Almanzo went to dances. They also liked to read books and magazines.

▼ **This is Laura and Almanzo's living room on Rocky Ridge Farm.**

Becoming a Writer

Laura and Almanzo's daughter Rose was a talented and independent young woman. She became a writer and moved to California. Rose remembered the many stories her mother had told her. Laura made life as a pioneer girl come alive. Rose convinced her mother to write a book about her early life. Laura was in her sixties when she wrote *Pioneer Girl*. It was about pioneer life with Pa and Ma.

Laura Ingalls Wilder

◀ This is the writing desk Laura used when she lived on Rocky Ridge Farm.

Later, Rose and Laura rewrote her original book. It was published as *Little House in the Big Woods*.

Laura wrote eight more books about life on the frontier. Her books have been published in more than 40 languages. Children all over the world love her books. She died in 1957, three days after her 90th birthday.

Planes, Trains, and Automobiles

Laura lived long enough to ride in covered wagons, trains, cars, and even airplanes. She once took an airplane to California to visit Rose. While there, she fulfilled a lifelong dream to see the ocean.

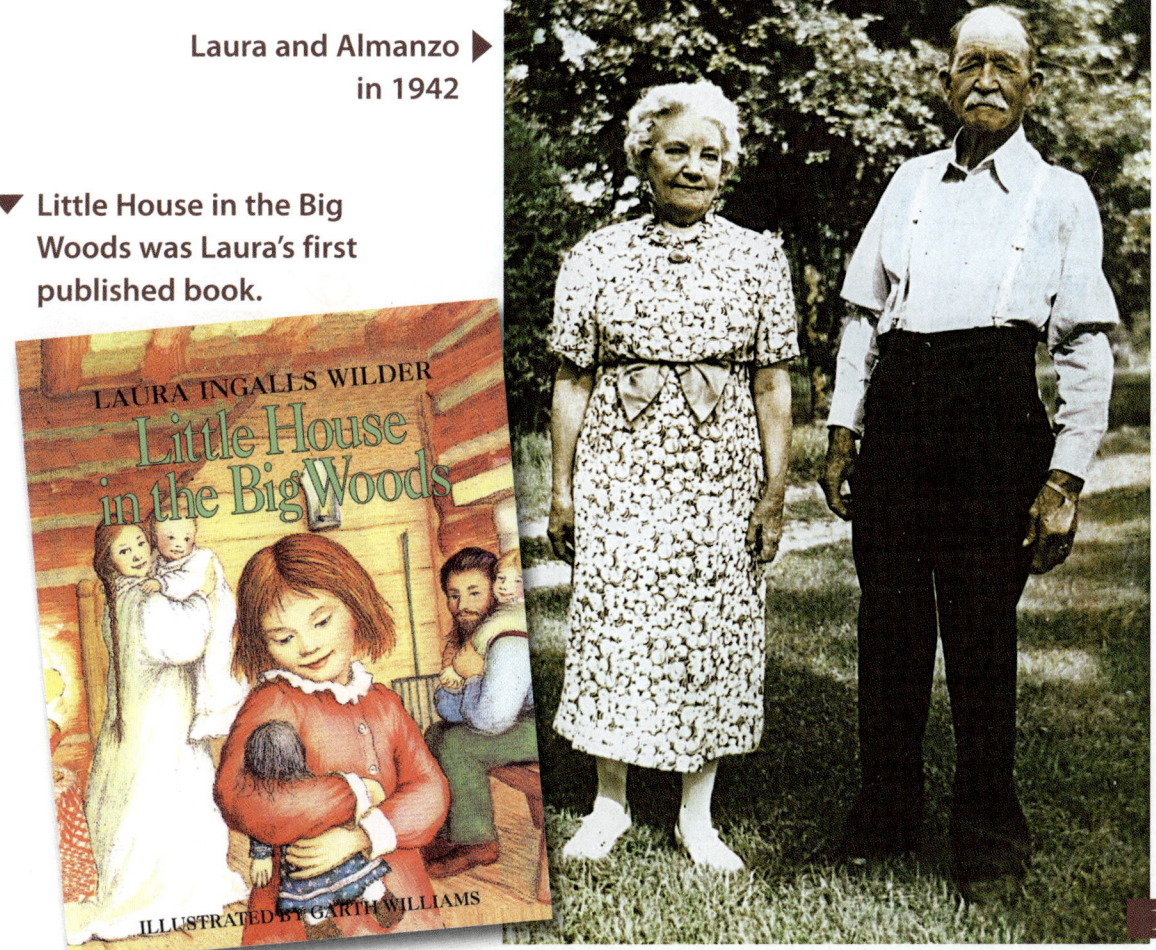

▶ **Laura and Almanzo in 1942**

▼ **Little House in the Big Woods was Laura's first published book.**

Pioneer Women

Laura Ingalls Wilder is a well-known pioneer woman because she wrote about her life. Many pioneer women helped change life in the United States. The following pages tell how these brave women survived in the West.

The First Pioneer Woman

In 1836, Narcissa Whitman traveled west with her husband Marcus. They were **missionaries**. They wanted to share their Christian beliefs with the American Indians. Narcissa was one of the first white women to travel along the Oregon Trail. The Whitmans set up a mission in what is now Washington State.

▼ The Whitman mission around 1847

Tragedy Strikes

Life in the West was not easy for Narcissa. She became very sad after her daughter drowned. She also missed other family members who still lived in the East.

Narcissa Whitman ▶ tried to help sick Cayuse Indians.

Narcissa spent much of her time working with the Cayuse (KI-yoos) Indians. She taught them how to farm and raise cattle. She also shared her Christian beliefs with them.

In 1847, there was a terrible **measles** (MEE-zuhlz) outbreak. The American Indians got very sick. Many Cayuse children died. The Cayuse blamed Narcissa and her family. They said she had poisoned the children. In anger, the Cayuse killed Narcissa, her husband, and 20 other pioneers.

Pioneer Women (cont.)

A Woman's Life on the Trail

"All of our work requires **stooping**," complained one female pioneer. There were no tables or chairs set up in camp. So, women always had to bend over or stand as they worked.

Women dealt with a lot of hardships on the trail. Rain soaked their clothes and made it hard to cook. There was little time to sit and sew during the long days. So, clothes were made and mended at night in camp. A lot of work was done at night by candlelight.

Sometimes women even had to drive the wagons, herd cows, and build campfires. Along the trail, women also had to care for their children.

The whole family was involved in chores on the trail.

▼ The chores on the trail did not stop until late into the night.

Mary Ellen Pleasant

Black Pioneer Women

Many black women also moved west. Some slaves even gained their freedom in the Southwest where pioneers lived under Mexican law. Slavery was not allowed in land owned by Mexico. Mary Ellen Pleasant was an ex-slave who became wealthy in the West. She became a leading real estate dealer in California.

Pioneer Women (cont.)

Women Living in the West

Most homes in the West were made of tar paper, sod, or logs. Women were in charge of cleaning the homes. They also had to bring water to the houses from streams. Soap and clothes were handmade by women.

Women worked outside as well. They planted the gardens and fed the animals. Teachers were hard to find in the West. So, most women taught their children in their homes.

Pioneer women often said that life in the West was just as hard as life on the trail.

▲ This woman is making soap for her family.

▲ Women worked inside and outside their new homes in the West.

Stuck at Home

Most women did not get to leave their homes very often. Men would go into nearby towns to get goods. But, the women were expected to stay at home and take care of the children and the chores. With few neighbors, women often became very lonely.

◄ Women did not usually have to help build the homes. Instead, they helped by cooking for the men.

Pioneer Women (cont.)

Freedoms for Western Women

Women had more rights and freedoms in the West than they did in the East. They held jobs in the West that were thought to be men's jobs. Some women started their own businesses. They ran hotels and drove **stagecoaches**. Women mined for gold in California, too.

In 1869, women in Wyoming got the right to vote. It was not until 1920 that all women in the United States were allowed to vote.

▼ This stagecoach was headed into Dakota Territory in 1889.

▲ Women voting in Wyoming

Calamity Jane

Martha Jane Canary became a famous woman of the West. She and her parents moved to Utah when she was a child. As she grew up, she became a sharpshooter. Jane dressed as a man and could shoot while riding a horse. She traveled with Buffalo Bill's Wild West Show. She was known as Calamity Jane.

Many history books only tell about how the men experienced life along the frontier trails. It is important to realize that the pioneer women worked just as hard as the men. Laura Ingalls Wilder's stories have entertained generations of young people. Her stories have also helped people today see how pioneer women and their families survived the difficulties of living in the West.

Glossary

blizzards—storms with snow and strong winds

debt—owing money to someone

droughts—times with no rainfall

dugout—a home dug out of the earth, often located in a hill or creek bank

frontier—wilderness; unsettled area

homestead—the home and land a family worked on, after five years they owned it

livestock—animals kept for use or to make money

malaria—a disease caused by mosquitoes

measles—a disease that causes fever and a rash

missionaries—people who work to change someone to their beliefs

polio—a disease of the nerves that makes one weak and sore

prairie—a grassy area with no trees

rivals—two people that compete hoping to beat each other

sharpshooter—someone good at shooting a gun

sod—mixture made out of thick grass and dirt

stagecoaches—horse-drawn wagons used to carry people or mail in the West

stooping—bending over

territory—areas of land controlled by a country that lie outside the country's borders